Empath

A Self-Discovery Journey for Highly Sensitive People to Gain Control over Emotions, overcome Negative Mindsets and develop Self-Confidence

by David Larson

ISBN: 9781075037528

Table of Contents

Introduction

Welcome, humble reader, and congratulations on taking your first step toward discovering who and what you really are. In order to truly accept ourselves, we need to understand who we are and what we're capable of. With this book, we're going to learn about empathy together. We are going to cover all the benefits of being an empath and how you can use these to your advantage. Naturally, there are some disadvantages to being an empath, which I am sure you have already experienced, and we're going to cover the best ways to overcome these downfalls to make your life more positive overall.

You may be aware that you are an empath or you may be looking to find out what an empath is. Perhaps you know that you've always been attuned to other people's emotions and feelings, perhaps someone said the word and it got you thinking, or perhaps you stumbled upon it all on your own. Whether you are an empath or you know someone else who is an empath, the contents of this book will help with several different things regarding this gift. That's what empathy is: a gift.

Empaths have a massive amount of potential, but not all of them know how to release this potential. I'm going to show you how to do that. If you want to do that, however, you need to realize how incredibly crucial it is to accept yourself. I know it's a lot easier said than done. That's another thing I hope to help you within this book. This journey is not one of mere self-discovery, but of self-acceptance and self-improvement. Once you've accepted being an empath, along with all its pros and cons, you can use that gift to unlock your full potential and live your best life. You will no longer fight the gift you have. Instead, you'll use it to your advantage. With self-acceptance and self-improvement, we can accomplish this.

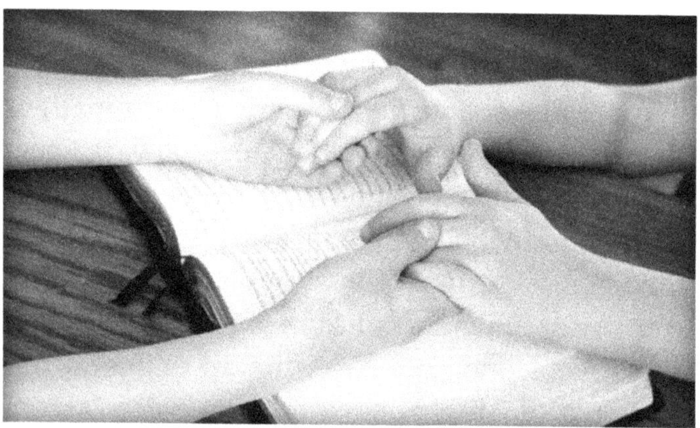

The first thing I need to tell you is that while an empath is highly sensitive, it is not a bad thing.

Often, this gift can feel like a burden and a struggle rather than a good thing. I can promise you right now, you're not being "too sensitive," as some would say. The ability to feel things deeply—even when they are not necessarily yours to feel—is a gift. I know that it may make things difficult sometimes. You may not always understand why you're feeling things as intensely as you are. Regardless, I'm going to show you why it's a gift. I'm going to tell you all about empathy so that you can better understand what that gift is. And most importantly, I'm going to show you how to use this gift to thrive in life, rather than allow it to bring you down.

In the end, empathy is a skill that you can use in lots of different aspects of life. It can help you form deeper bonds with people, it can inform you of when to stay away from others, and it can give you a boost of self-confidence. All you need to do is learn how to use it to your advantage. That's where I come in. Consider this book a guide of sorts, one that will help you discover yourself and overcome negative emotions, as well as push you to be more confident in life.

You know what they say, confidence is attractive. There is more than one form of attractiveness.

Sure, everyone likes looking good, and if you feel good, that *does* come through. However, I'm referring to emotional, mental, and universal attraction. Once you're confident with yourself and this gift of yours, good things are bound to come your way. They may be in the form of opportunities, they may be in the form of romance, and they may be in the form of friendships. Whatever the case may be, confidence will help you on your way to success.

Above all else, we'll also help you differentiate between the good and the bad things you attract. You know that niggling sensation you get in the back of your skull when something just doesn't sit right with you? You usually have no idea *why*. That's another good thing empathy brings your way. Our instincts as an empath are much stronger. It's important to learn how to identify these things and when to heed them as warnings. Let's be honest, not everyone and everything in this world is good. It's important to be able to tell when it's time to turn away from something and when you're letting your emotions get the better of you.

We're going to cover several things in this book, such as:

- What an empath actually is, from several

different perspectives, to help you better understand the gift of empathy.

- The best ways to preserve yourself and your empathic energy to prevent exhaustion, negative emotions, and burn-out.
- How you can thrive in your everyday life with the help of your gift.

Part One:

Empathy as the Gift

What Is an Empath?

You know how sometimes you tell a story and someone understands where you're coming from, so they say, "I feel you"? Well, empaths really, truly *do* feel you. They take it quite literally. If you are one of these people, then you may be an empath. You might even know someone else who seems to know exactly what you're feeling and thinking on a level no one else has ever managed to.

Empaths kind of have a super-ability. They can feel other people's emotions. Sometimes this goes to such an extent that they seem clairvoyant and/or able to read other people's minds. They understand emotions on a deeper basis, and in psychology, they are treated as a personality-type, but this makes their gift seem less rare than it actually is. You see, there are plenty of highly sensitive people in the world. There are people who are more attuned to the feelings of certain people. Empaths take this to the next notch and are often able to experience things such as the trauma of others as though it were their own.

Being an empath means that you are affected by other people's energy. This may unconsciously influence your own life as you have an inherent ability to perceive and feel the moods, thoughts, desires, wishes, and doubts of others. This is something that comes to empaths intuitively. It isn't limited to mere emotions and feelings; empaths can often feel the physical sensitivities of others, as well as what their intentions, motivations, and/or urges may be. It's not easily controlled, but it can be with a great effort of learning.

If you try to ignore your gift, you may end up causing a lot of inner chaos and confusion. Unfortunately, if you don't accept who you are and learn about how to control this gift, you can end up mistaking the way others feel as your own emotional turmoil. It's important to try to master your empathic abilities in order to avoid the negativity that can come with it. Many empaths feel as though their abilities are more of a curse than a blessing because they haven't learned about it. To them, this ability may seem as though outside energies are unwanted attacks and this can lead to a lot of bad symptoms, such as the overwhelming desire to escape.

However; being an empath isn't all bad. In fact, it can be wondrous. All it takes is some discovery.

You see, empaths are always open to process the energies and feelings of other people. Often, empaths take on the emotions of others. This can lead to a lot of adverse side-effects such as fatigue, unexplained pains, migraines, and environmental sensitivity contributed by outside influences. The unfortunate part about being an empath is that these things don't always come from an empath themselves. They are the accumulation of others. Imagine walking around with the feelings, emotions, and thoughts of thousands of other people. I don't know about you, but I feel like that would be a pretty exhausting burden to bear. If you're an empath, you probably know exactly what I'm talking about and you're wondering if there's any way out of this at all.

Worry not. There is. Being an empath, though it can feel heavy, is a gift. When you develop it, it can lead to wonderful things. One of the natural abilities that come with being an empath is healing abilities. Other benefits of the gift include a heightened sense of awareness, deep personal connections, and intense creativity. All that you need to unlock this potential is the knowledge of how to hone it.

I'm going to help you do exactly that, but first we're going to cover the different types of empaths.

The Different Types of Empath Personalities

Yes, there are different types of empaths. They aren't all bundled into one. Some of them have different abilities from one another, but one thing they have in common is a heightened sensitivity to those around them. Each empath personality type is normally stronger in one particular area of their ability. Their traits and senses may feel higher in different degrees. Sometimes, these are tied to spiritual beliefs and other times, they aren't.

Empaths have the unique ability of being able to

put themselves in someone else's shoes to the extent that they can feel what that person is feeling as though they actually are that person. It isn't easy. Often, empaths who don't know enough about their gift can find it tiring and confusing. Understanding the different types can help in identifying what abilities you have, and this can be used to help both yourself and those around you.

Remember that you can be more than one empath at a time. There are no limits. More often than not, empaths take on more than one different type of empathy, but they are often stronger in one or two areas.

Emotional Empath

This is one of the most common types of empaths. They deeply experience the emotions and feelings of others. I happen to be one of these, and if someone is sad or tired or angry, I feel that way almost instantly. This can be incredibly draining if you don't learn to differentiate between your own feelings and the feelings of others.

Consider this a bit like the flu. That sounds gross,

but that's essentially how it feels. It's almost as though you "caught" the emotions of another person generally within your vicinity. Sometimes it's even referred to as "emotional contagion" and other times, it's referred to as "personal distress."

Emotional empaths can understand and feel other people's emotions. This is a crucial skill for those in caring professions, like doctors and nurses. It allows them to read and respond to their patients in the best manner due to the fact that they can intuitively feel what their patients are going through. Of course, it isn't limited to profession. This is a great skill for anyone to have, especially if you want to help loved ones when they are in personal distress.

You don't have to be an empath to be there for someone, but it certainly helps.

The way an emotional empath works is by sensing and absorbing the emotions and energies of others. They can feel these things to the extent that, whether it's obvious or not, they can automatically tell when someone is in a good or a bad mood. The empath will almost always feel exactly the same way, and they won't ever have to ask how the other person is feeling. Naturally, this means that it's harder for people to pretend around an emotional empath. The empath will be able to see through this and feel what the other person is really feeling. So if you know an empath, don't bother lying to them about your bad mood because the odds are, they felt it the moment they walked into the same room.

Something to keep in mind with emotional empathy is that you don't need to know the people around you to be able to feel what they feel. They don't need to say anything for you to catch their emotions. Heartbreak can sometimes be so intense that it causes a physical ache in the chest accompanied by a deep sadness. Emotional empaths will be able to feel *both* these aches.

Physical Empath

This one is rarer and heard of far less frequently. As the title would suggest, these empaths have the ability to physically feel another person's pain and/or illness when they are in the same vicinity. It sounds impossible to some, but this is a legitimate awareness of what symptoms someone else is experiencing.

As an example, a physical empath can actually feel the same pain or symptoms in their own body. That might sound awful, but it can actually be a fantastic skill to have if you need to know exactly what is wrong with someone. Imagine a doctor with the ability of physical empathy; they'd be able to pinpoint the exact location of the pain and, depending on how strong their ability is, the severity of the problem their patient is experiencing. Physical empaths can make excellent healers as they often sense what the other person will need, be it a headache tablet or something to up their energy levels.

Needless to say, this type of empathy makes for a fantastic healing professional. This can either be a conventional medical profession such as a doctor or an alternative practitioner such as a shaman. These empaths can feel a sense of heightened awareness within their own body when they treat someone. As a result, they can also feel the blockages within a person's field of energy, which is something often found in homeopathy such as acupuncture. The intuition in this type of empathy is strong enough that the empath picks up on the energy of another person and uses it to tell what ails the other person.

Naturally, taking on the physical ailments of others can lead to health problems. If you are this type of empath, it would be best to take some kind of training in order to hone your skills. This will help you switch off the ability when necessary.

Intuitive/Clairvoyant Empath

Most empaths have clairvoyant abilities, but some empaths *only* have these abilities. As such, it is much stronger within such individuals. It means that they can pick up a great deal of insight from someone else by merely being within their presence. These empaths are often able to tell exactly when someone is lying to them as well as having a distinctive sense of knowing. They're highly perceptive of the intentions of others, whether open or secretive.

Sometimes, these empaths have predictive dreams. They often feel like they experience déjà vu on a regular basis as a result. Their dreams can actually become a reality in the following days, months, and sometimes years.

Intuitive empathy is very closely related to telepathic empathy, in which the empath can read another person's thoughts. They are often grouped together, as I am currently grouping them together. The gift allows these empaths to read the energy of other people easily. In this case, it is important to learn how to strengthen your own energy in order to protect yourself from the thoughts of others. These empaths have the strongest sense of intuition without ever needing to be given certain information or knowledge.

These empaths should take care to surround themselves with people they feel united with.

Animal/Fauna Empath

Yeah, they exist. I'm sure you've already figured out where this is going.

The animal/fauna empath will have a strong connection to animals, and animals may be more drawn to them, meaning that they might be the type of person who works with and takes care of animals for the rest of their life. In such cases, the empath may be able to telepathically communicate with animals and/or know exactly what they need when they need it.

These empaths are the whisperers of the world. We've all heard of them: dog whisperers, cat whisperers, and horse whisperers. They love the animals they make connections with. Sometimes they prefer the company of their furry—or not-so-furry—friends to that of people. I mean, I can't say I blame them.

Animal empaths tend to spend a lot of time with animals. They may even feel their energies recharged by being near animals. Studying animals can help refine this gift. If it's a profession you wish to enter into, consider training as an animal healer. There's never too many in this world, and the special gift will allow you to figure out what is wrong with an animal and how to treat it quickly.

Plant/Flora Empath

Green thumbs of the world unite!

Plant empaths have a strong link to nature and love being surrounded by it. So, too, plants will thrive in their presence. I'm sure you're beginning to notice that the pull to empaths goes both ways. In this case, the empath knows exactly what plants need and offer, which is why they're so affectionately known as having green thumbs. They intuitively know how to tend to any type of greenery, and if it's a plant they're unfamiliar with, they pick up on it quickly.

A great benefit of being a plant empath is the awareness that comes with it. These empaths have the ability to naturally knowing what is edible and what isn't. They can also tell what the environment needs in order to maintain balance. Generally, those who go into professional occupations involving plants are plant empaths. They might even hear the voices of trees or plants, claiming that nature guides them in what they do.

An excellent way to strengthen this bond is by simply sitting quietly in nature near a special tree or plant and aligning yourself closely to it and its needs.

Environmental/Geomantic Empath

Now, these empaths are closely related to plant empaths in the fact that they are environmentally inclined. They have the gift of sensing that which may happen or has already happened in certain places, such as the ability to tell when volcanoes are going to erupt. They are finely attuned to physical landscapes. If you're someone who is really happy or otherwise unhappy in certain environments, you might be one of these.

Generally, these empaths can read a space, as psychometric empaths can read physical objects. They become sensitive to something that may have happened or will happen in that space. This can be so deep that if they pick up certain objects, they can actually learn about the previous owner(s).

Pulls to powerful places accompany this sense of empathy. Geomantic empaths may like places such as churches, sacred stones, and/or groves. Naturally, this means they may also be sensitive to the history of such locations. Due to their connection to the world, they grieve the damage it suffers. If you are this type of empath, you can recharge by spending time in nature. Consider taking on projects to help the earth and/or the environment if you are ever in need of extra healing.

Surround yourself with natural scents and materials to strengthen your energy and happiness.

Spiritual/Medium Empath

The odds are that you've heard about mediums and their connection with the deceased or other spiritual entities and beings. Spiritual empaths often have direct links to other realms and plains. Consider it a psychic empathic ability.

This type of empathy is similar to that of emotional empathy in that they have a connection to others. The only difference is that emotional empaths have a connection to the physical world, whilst spiritual empaths have more of a connection to those in the spiritual world. Naturally, this depends strongly on beliefs. There are some people who are highly skeptical of this sort of empathy due to not believing in the existence of a spiritual world, let alone the idea of someone being able to feel the physical and emotional symptoms from it.

These empaths may not always be able to see, feel, *and* hear. Their senses can be limited to one. As any horror film will indicate, this level of hearing, feeling, or sight can be frightening. It's strongly recommended that people with this type of empathy train and learn of its benefits. It can be controlled and should be in order for the empaths to be able to properly protect themselves.

Heyoka Empath

Okay, I'm not going to lie to you. This one is a bit weird. You may have seen them without ever knowing their names in films.

This is a Native American term used to describe a trickster or an unconventional go-between. They have the ability to move between the physical and spiritual realms acting as a psychic medium to communicate in between the two worlds. They absorb feelings and emotions with the specific intention of mirroring it back to a person. In doing so, they can show others what they need to see.

Heyoka empaths are incredibly rare and are generally raised with the knowledge of what they are, as it is a common occupation in Native American culture. This is an ancient form of empathy. These empaths have an uncanny ability to speak to people in such a way that the person they're speaking to will almost immediately be able to see their situation in a different light than before.

They often use humor to help heal people.

The Differences Between Empathy, Sympathy, and Compassion

These three words are terms that many people

use interchangeably, but that doesn't mean they're all the same thing. That can be confusing because they all have similar meanings. However, they are not synonyms.

Empathy is the ability to *feel* what a person is feeling. Sympathy is the ability to *understand* what a person is feeling. Compassion is the want to *relieve* those feelings, particularly if they are negative or suffering.

Let's go over this more in-depth to properly understand the differences between each one.

Empathy

We've already covered a rather large portion of this definition, but to put it simply, it's the visceral feeling of what another person feels. That being said, empathy can arise the moment you see someone in pain due to mirror neurons even if you aren't an empath. These mirror neurons kick in and reflect someone else's pain back at you. Have you ever watched someone hurt themselves and immediately felt the same pain? Those are the mirror neurons working.

Sometimes we have to rely on our imagination rather than actually feeling the pain of someone else. The idea of putting yourself in someone else's shoes is what being an empath is all about. Empathizing is the ability to imagine what someone else is going through, whereas an empath simply does it naturally.

The empathic feelings can be good too. How many times does a stranger laughing or smiling elicit the same reaction out of you? I think we've all been there.

Sympathy

It's a bit more difficult to differentiate between sympathy and empathy. When one experiences sympathy, they are not experiencing how another feels. They are simply able to understand that pain, either due to relating to it on a personal level or by using cognitive skills to recognize what makes that person feel that way. For example, if a friend has lost a pet and you haven't, you don't know what they're going through, but you have either felt it before and/or you have the ability to understand how upsetting that would be.

Sympathizing with a person is simply a way of letting someone else know that their suffering is recognized and that they are not alone.

Compassion

Compassion is almost like a combination of empathy and sympathy, combined with the choice to take it an extra step further. Not only do you feel the pain of another person and/or recognize it, you also choose to do your best to alleviate that person's pain. You have the desire to make them feel better about their situation.

Practicing compassion means being in the moment of suffering. It literally comes from the roots of Latin, "to suffer with." In such instances, you deliberately choose not to run away from the suffering and you don't allow it to overwhelm you. An example of compassion is simply listening. Have you ever listened to someone else talk about their problems or had someone else listen to you talk about yours? The compassionate thing to do would be to simply listen without judging rather than attempting to solve your problem or turning it back to themselves by relating to it. The simple act of listening to someone can be one of the most compassionate things you can ever do for someone.

Be aware that constantly feeling the pain of another can lead to burnout. Empathy fatigue is a very real thing, commonly associated with caregivers and healthcare providers. This is where the distinction between empathy and compassion come in; compassion won't usually affect your wellbeing, whereas empathy can. That being said, compassion is renewable. If you help someone by alleviating their suffering, you are actually less likely to burn out.

Compassion and empathy activate different regions of the brain. It has been proven that compassion can fight against empathetic distress. Turns out, compassion is actually a medicine in more than one way.

The Pros and Cons of Being an Empath

Depending how long you've known that you are an empath, you may be quite familiar with the pros and cons of being one. We've already covered that one of the downfalls can be the way it is a heavy burden to bear due to the outside energies and emotions you are surrounded by. However, most things in life come with both negatives and positives. The experience of feeling those emotions around you can be wonderful and helpful in many different ways.

The pros and cons can't really be separated as they are often intertwined with one another.

Empaths are listeners. They can be all sorts of joy, being outgoing and enthusiastic and generally bubbly. Let's not forget the heyoka empath literally known for being humorous when you least expect it. Their journey can be one of emotional bliss, but it can also be one of emotional turmoil since empaths can be weighed down with mood swings galore. This is because their moods are not always their own. If empaths don't fully understand and differentiate their own thoughts and feelings from those of others, they can have fluctuating mood swings that literally change with the speed of flicking a switch on and off.

As with the good, being an empath can come with feelings of depression, anxiety, panic, fear, and sorrow. Without having any control over these feelings, you can be experiencing the suffering of others. It's a very difficult thing to have to handle and shouldn't be done so alone.

This is where compassion comes in. An empath should have at least one person they can turn to in the throes of these mood swings because being left alone can be detrimental to mental and physical health. Find someone, be it a friend or a partner or a family member, who you can turn to when things get too overwhelming for you. Whoever you find, make sure to tell them that all you really need from them is empathic love—the ability to show compassion without judging you. This may help you in recovery from these overwhelming moments.

Most empaths, unless they have gone on their own journeys of self-discovery and self-acceptance, don't actually know or understand what's going on within. They don't know that they're feeling another person's emotions like they are their own emotions. This can quite obviously lead to a myriad of feelings such as confusion, particularly if things were grand in one moment and terrible in the next. Understanding their empathic connection is a part of the journey.

It's easier for an empath to withhold their feelings and emotions than it is for others. They want to do their best not to be barraged by the feelings and emotions of others. In doing so, they often become reclusive and learn to block out these feelings. The downside of this is that they can end up bottling up their own emotions or building walls so high that they don't ever let anyone else in. This can definitely be bad for an empath—or anyone for that matter—because the longer you allow these feelings and emotions to build up inside yourself, the more power they build up. Eventually, they can explode and leave behind a lot of damage to both the empath and those around the empath. This can create an unstable environment, a mental/emotional breakdown, and/or an actual disease.

Expressing yourself honestly is a choice, but it is a great form of healing.

Cons of Being an Empath

Some of these can count as pros depending on how you look at them. You'll notice how short this list is compared to the list of pros. This is because being an empath is truly a positive blessing if you understand your gift properly.

- You are easily overwhelmed. I've mentioned this a few times over, but it is probably the biggest downside to being an empath. Wherever there are lots of people, you can be overwhelmed with the feelings and emotions emanating off of those that surround you. Sometimes you can be in a room with one person and still feel this way. This is why it is so important not to bottle things up.

- Addictive personalities. Empaths are prone to looking for ways to escape or block out the emotions of others. This means that they sometimes turn toward addictive substances such as sex, drugs, and alcohol. Learning to protect yourself and your energy means that you won't be struck with the need to escape these things. Instead, you will know how to cope with them properly.

- Media can be devastating. Some empaths turn away from media altogether. They can feel the emotions of others so strongly that even reading a newspaper is too much for them. It is a harsh world out there.

- Empaths can pick up both mental and physical ailments that others may suffer from. This can happen even if you don't come into contact with the other person, depending on how strong your gift is. Needless to say, no one wants to suffer this way.

- Intuition can be hurtful when you know that someone you care about is lying to you or keeping secrets from you. The ability to know and feel these things can be difficult, particularly if you can't prove such things. Try to surround yourself with people who are like minded to prevent feeling this way on a regular basis.

- We don't really have a home. Empaths are natural wanderers. After a certain amount of time, we can often feel foreign in places we once cherished. Our intuition implores with us to explore the great big world. Due to this, we're rarely ever satisfied with one place, but it does mean we make brilliant travelers.

Pros of Being an Empath

Well, we covered the cons, which I admit were pretty bad. Now we get to look at the reasons why being an empath truly is a gift. Bear with me here, because it's a pretty long list of reasons.

- Empaths are natural healers in many different forms: emotional, physical, environmental, animal, you name it. They can use their touch, their voice, and their creativity to do so. Most empaths end up on a path of healing because they simply have that pull toward their profession.

- As tough as crowds may be for an empath, the small circle they often end up building for themselves is a strong one. Once an empath makes a connection with someone, they are incredibly loyal and loving. We hold onto our loved ones tightly because we don't want to let the good ones go.

- Okay, we already know this one, but empaths love an insane amount. Their hearts are just bigger than most. Being so overloaded with all these feelings makes faking them difficult.

- That gut instinct is extremely strong and if you listen to it, I'm pretty sure you could conquer the world if you wanted to. As an empath, I often ignore my intuition, and it has never been wrong, so I'm working on listening to it more often. Listen to that sixth sense of yours because it could save you from potential dangers if it hasn't already.

- Along with having an extremely strong sense of intuition, we also have amazing senses. It isn't only emotions and feelings that are heightened. If you find yourself enjoying a myriad of sensations with a lot more intensity than those around you, you can chalk that up to being an empath. We have heightened senses that allow us to better enjoy our food, beverages, flowers, essential oils, touch, and so forth. Admittedly, these can sometimes overwhelm us, but they could also help save lives. How, you might ask? Well, if you work on increasing a certain sense, such as smell, you could be able to track down death or disease in animals, people, and/or nature.

- I know we said that the weight of other people's emotions is a burden and we're really prone to lows, but we've also got the other end of the spectrum. We have great highs, too. Most empaths actually have a deep enthusiasm for life, and when we are enjoying it, we experience joy intensely.

- Empaths have an abundance of creativity! I've mentioned this, but wow, it deserves a point all its own. We think and see things differently. Our art is not the only creative aspect of our life, but so are our experiences, situations, and prospects. Now, you've probably had the misfortune of being told that the way you think about and/or do things is wrong, but it's a capacity all your own. Don't let anyone take that unusual creativity away from you, and let it shine brightly instead.

- This Is yet another con that also turns out to be a pro, but we can't be lied to. We are good at reading people's thoughts, feelings, and emotions. This means that we can tell when people are lying, we can tell when people aren't okay, and we can tell when people are bad news.

- Empaths can read emotional and nonverbal cues really well. It's a talent in numerous places. Due to our good senses, we can even sense the needs of those who do not speak, such as animals and plants, but also the body and babies.

- An empath generally has a craving to make the world a better place. This isn't a desire that you should ever feel ashamed of. We are capable of bringing plenty of positive changes to this world, and when we can, we should. There are already too many people turning blind eyes. Let's work on correcting the wrongs happening around us—together.

- It's especially important for us to change the world considering our pull to it. We are children of nature. It's one of the best ways to de-stress, and it can provide peace and comfort.
- To some, this might seem more like a con, but I find that it's pretty cool to be able to recharge on our own. We require a certain level of alone time to recuperate. It is because of this that we are self-aware, and I think it's great to be self-aware.

How Empaths Can Understand and Help Other People

I've already mentioned this, but I want to give you a deeper insight into how empaths can help people. We've already established that they're drawn to healing and bear the type of personality that wants the world to be a better place, but how do they go about making it one? Sure, compassion is a huge part of empathy, but what else can they do? I'd be happy to tell you.

The good that an empath wishes to do—or, rather, is *capable* of doing—is quite dependent on what type of empath they are. Naturally, pardon the pun, the environmental/geomantic empath has more of a pull to fix the earth. This is the same for the plant/flora empath. When an empath homes their gifts, they can use them to maintain balance and restore harmony into the world. They have their own unique ways of doing this.

Empaths are fantastic listeners. They genuinely care about and enjoy learning about others, mostly because they can feel the emotions of the other person. There's a sort of rush you feel when someone tells you their stories as it can feel as though you were actually there. When someone needs support, an empath can perceive that and provide it accordingly. The empath can sense things like fear or danger, and if they've strengthened their gifts or are attuned to them, they can use the skills and adaptations they've developed to remove themselves and others from such a situation. They don't talk about themselves much, but if they do, it reveals that they have a great deal of trust in the person they're sharing with. Often, however, people seem to trust them quickly. This is because they relate to others in their own unique way.

It is because of this relatability that people feel a pull toward empaths. It doesn't matter if the empath is aware of their empathic abilities; people will still be drawn to them. People are willing to pour their hearts and souls out to empaths who are complete strangers without necessarily intending to do so. It happens on a subconscious level.

Needless to say, sometimes the empath needs that release too. That's why it's imperative that they find some of their own kind or they keep those special friends close. They're exceptional people.

Another way empaths use their abilities to bring good into the world is the ability to solve problems. Since they enjoy learning as much as they do, they study many things, and this means they are constantly sharpening their minds. Sometimes this is a subconscious action. The empath brings new meaning to the saying: "Where there is a will, there is a way."

Though it helps others, you should be wary of the fact that people will often want to offload their problems onto you. These people might not even know you. If you don't keep your guard up and strengthen your energy, these problems can convert into being *your* problems. Make sure that you keep the two separate. You don't want to be dragged on. Be honest with yourself and others. If a situation feels like it is going to bring negativity your way, it is okay to take a step back and tell the other person that you can't handle it. This is an act of self-preservation.

I know that sometimes it might feel like you are thrown into scenarios aimlessly and in them, you drink up the emotions of others, but you are stronger than you think. Empaths *have* to be strong to be able to carry both their own feelings and the feelings of others. Consider yourself a type of energy warrior. You absorb all this energy and transform it into something valuable. You have the ability to shift the negative to positive. Purify the world. If anyone can do it, an empath can.

Remember how I said compassion is one of the best ways for an empath to avoid emotional distress? Some empaths find that they need to be in a constant state of compassion in order not to suffer adverse effects from outside influences. Others try to be as open as they can be, allowing each feeling and sensation to pass through without much notice, and in doing so, they release all judgment and try to be as honest and carefree as possible. Then there are the empaths who believe in crystal healing in order to transfer and create energetic healing. The empath who heals the world in whatever manner they need to is the empath who has a great sense of inner peace and balance because they know that they are following their calling in life.

If you've already found what you're meant to be doing—say, for instance, mine is releasing my creativity into the world in any manner I deem appropriate—then you know what I mean by feeling a sense of balance. If you're still looking, don't give up. Follow your intuition and it won't lead you astray. Bear in mind that you may fail a few times. You may think that you've found that thing you're meant to be doing only to realize that it was nothing more than a step toward where you're meant to be. Keep searching even when you hit this wall. You are on the journey you are following for a reason. That reason will reveal itself to you soon. An empath's gut is usually right.

Part Two:

Self-Discovery,

Self-Acceptance, and

Self-Improvement

Within this section of the book, we are going to cover a set of important tips that will help you preserve yourself and your energy, which is something I am sure you have come to realize you need to do as an empath.

Honest Self-Analysis

The first thing you need to keep in mind is that not everyone is an empath. It is a natural ability that is unique in the fact that it is something you are born with. Whilst people can have empathy, being an empath is not something that can be taught. There are plenty of people in the world who cannot feel what others feel, nor can they imagine putting themselves in another person's situation. Then again, there are plenty who handle the feelings of humans, animals, plants, places, and spirits every day of their lives.

Once you discover what you are as an empath, you may find yourself realizing who you are and why you do certain things. You may believe that you don't fit in with others because they treat you as being strange. In a way, they're right. You *are* strange because you *are* different, but that doesn't mean it's a bad thing. The way you see and feel things is different from the way most people see and feel things. You may find yourself standing out.

It's Okay to Be Different

Now, it's natural of humans to want to fit in, but being different comes with the territory of being an empath. That's not to say that you'll never fit in. In fact, there is a place where you belong and that is among other empaths. Yes, they are out there and they do understand you. You may never be able to fit in with the majority, but you *can* fit in with the minority, and there is nothing wrong with that. It only makes you more special.

Standing out in your daily life can be challenging and draining, particularly when you think about the fact that you are feeling the emotions of others. These things do not belong to you. It's vital that you understand that much.

I know that explaining the stresses that this skill brings you can seem impossible too. Remember that what's normal to you may not be normal to someone else and vice versa. After all, what is normal for the spider is chaos for the fly. You don't need everyone to understand you so long as you understand you. If you realize that this gift is something that not everyone will understand, but it's something that you accept as a part of yourself, you are already miles ahead of the crowd behind you.

What Is It Like Being an Empath?

Pro Tip: Find someone of your own kind.

Look, they're not as difficult to find as it might seem. With the world so reliant on technology, the internet, and social media, it's actually a lot easier to find other empaths. There are sites, forums, and groups for you to join. In them, you will find more like-minded people. It can be incredibly therapeutic and helpful to find someone who actually understands you and doesn't look at you like you're on some kind of illegal substance because we all know how difficult it is to explain what it's like to be an empath. Don't we?

An added benefit of being in the world today is that not only can you find other empaths, but you can find your specific type of empath. You can connect with someone who is an emotional empath or a physical empath or a plant empath if that's who you are. All it takes is typing a few words into the search bar.

Once you find your people, you'll feel less secluded because the truth is, being an empath is almost exactly like being a normal person. It's not as though you want to go and live in nature on an abandoned island or protest against things like tree cutting (though those may be things that you're interested in doing). No, it simply means that you've got a deeper connection to the world and the people around you.

That's what it's really like to be an empath.

Finding Yourself as An Empath

The moment you realize who and what you are, you might find things falling into place. This is because you might discover things that accompany the gifts of an empath. A good example is the love of creativity. Most empaths are creative and they enjoy doing things like writing or playing music in order to calm their thoughts and make their minds feel like a home of their own rather than a home to all the external influences of people and the world.

Let me tell you about the secret of empaths. They are beautiful creatures. They adore healing people, plants, and animals. They love with such depth and intensity that they could actually move entire planets when accepted for who they are. Empaths are unique and talented. Sure, they can carry the weight of the world on their shoulders, but it's important to come to terms with the fact that as heavy as that world feels, it's also a brilliant thing.

I'm pretty sure we can all agree on that front.

As an empath, you need to come to terms with the fact that it is not up to you to fix everything. The world can be noisy too. Sometimes all you need is to take a step back, find your personal space, and sit in it calmly. Do whatever it takes to recharge and never compromise your recharge time for anyone or anything else. This is one of the mistakes that an empath can make. They forget to take care of themselves because they're so busy taking care of everyone and everything else.

I don't need to tell you that it can be tough to find a partner in this life. The person you find will either be an empath or an extremely compassionate person. They might become a source of comfort to you. They'll be the person who can calm you down without trying to fix your life for you. By now, you know that you aren't alone. I can assure you that you are not crazy for experiencing things the way that you do. And, believe it or not, that person is somewhere out there.

If you're lucky enough to have met your partner, I hope that you always let them know how much they mean to you and that they are always there to steady you in times where the external influences get overwhelming.

The Benefits of Self-Analysis

There are few skills more valuable and vital to the path of self-improvement than being able to take an honest look at oneself. If you reflect on yourself often and make a habit of it, you can expose any problems early on, making them easier to repair before they become mountains. Stop them while they are molehills.

As important as it is to be able to evaluate oneself honestly, it is admittedly one of the more difficult skills to master. We're human and that means that we're rather conceited by nature. We don't want to look at the bad parts of ourselves, so we tend to shy away from that. In my experience, empaths actually find a lot more faults within and of themselves than most people do. Regardless, the idea of looking into a mirror that could reveal a distorted version of ourselves is rather terrifying.

Below, I'm going to list some of the benefits to honest self-analysis.

- False confidence is a real thing. It corrupts the ability to make changes. Unfortunately, many people suffer from the affliction of false confidence. It allows them to believe that they don't need to improve—the thought that you are wealthier than you actually are can leave you scraping the barrel at the end of the month rather than focusing on goals and success. In order to relieve yourself of false confidence, you need to be able to be honest with yourself. This is the power of truthful reflection. Don't lie to yourself. It only distorts the image in the mirror looking back at you.

- I know it can be tempting to do your best to avoid failure, but the truth is that that isn't really the way that you succeed. Your level of success depends more on the ability to actually recover from the failures. You have already shown that you are capable of greatness by simply getting back up and saying, "Okay, I failed. I know where I went wrong. I'm ready to try again."

- Demanding honesty from your self-evaluations is the best way to scrap any blind optimism and false confidence. It's not an easy feat, but if you practice it, you can master it. I'm not going to lie to you; true, honest self-analysis is hard. It is uncomfortable, particularly when you look at the negative aspects. You can't give up hope though. You only end up adding more distortion to the reflection if you do that. Honesty is the first step you have to take before you can actually make alterations to the evaluations you make. Once you've done that, you'll see that it wasn't a pessimistic action at all. It was a path toward true optimism.

- If you write whatever comes to mind, your empathic intuition will steer you in the right direction. You have to do it immediately to get the best benefits. Most distortions happen when you leave things to sit and you've spent time thinking about them rather than simply getting them out. Don't censor your thoughts or your ideas because they don't fit what you want. A lot of the things you write are going to seem like trash, but that makes them easier to filter through at the end of it. This is beneficial because you'll notice some honest reflections you hadn't even considered before.

- A truly honest evaluation will allow you to remove yourself from the situation, which can help an empath in many ways. The primary way is that you learn emotional distance. This can stop emotions from overwhelming you and changing the impressions you have of yourself. Take a day off a week and do a review of how far you've come. This is particularly important if you have big decisions to make—I mean so big that they change your life for durations as long as years. You'll get a lot of clarity by taking those days off. You might even come up with new evaluations, but it's important to stick to the day off. Your mind, your senses, and your emotions need that.

Every person has taken one or more wrong paths in their lives. In order to succeed, we generally have to first fail. Mistakes are meant to be learned from. That's one of the amazing things about being human. We have the ability to learn from our mistakes. That's the key to finding yourself on the right path.

Be honest with yourself and you'll notice how little time you waste on dead ends and the bottoms of barrels.

Analyzing Yourself

Below are some helpful ways to analyze yourself. You may be asking why that's necessary. Well, analyzing ourselves means that we can better assess the way we react to certain reactions. In some cases, the way we react could do with tweaking, but we won't know what to change if we don't know what we're doing wrong in the first place. Keep an open mind. This is all about self-improvement.

Remember that you want to analyze the way you react in all environments rather than one.

- Speak to someone you trust. Sometimes the best way to get a gauge on our behavior is by asking someone else about it. Sit down and ask them to tell you honestly how they feel about you and where they believe improvements can be made. It's important not to let anything they say upset you. They might not feel comfortable enough to be honest with you in the future if you react adversely.

- Define where being an empath could be a problem. This could be at home, at work, with your family, during social interactions, or with strangers. Once you've established the points you struggle with, you can come up with some coping mechanisms, such as repeating a few positive affirmations when you feel things getting difficult or learning to take a voluntary step back.

- Try journaling. You can keep a dream journal, a day journal, and/or a work journal. Take down all of the things you feel and think without leaving anything out.
- Meditate or do yoga. These are great ways of clearing the mind. Sometimes that's exactly what you need to do when things become overwhelming.
- Art! Yes, creating art can help. There are various resources such as doodle books that allow you to analyze how you feel using imagery.

Self-Assessment Questionnaire

This is going to be a quiz of sorts. The questions

I'm going to ask you will determine whether or not you exhibit the main traits of an empath. These questions aren't going to guarantee that you *are* an empath, but if you find yourself relating to them as well as the rest of this book, then you very well may be one.

By now, if you weren't before, you are well aware of the fact that it is not always easy to be an empath. Knowing that you are and what type you are will help you keep your own space and boundaries. I am going to include methods of self-care in order for you to remain balanced, should you exhibit any of the traits defined.

1. Are you able to correctly guess what others are thinking on a regular basis?

Empaths are often able to sync up with people to the extent that they can complete people's sentence or reflect their personalities. Generally, there needs to be some sort of connection between the two of you, but that isn't always the case. This is why it sometimes seems like empaths are able to read people's minds.

This is something that can happen to anyone, but it is far more common that empaths will see a pattern. It's not necessarily a bad thing, but you should protect yourself from absorbing too much of other people. It could lead to burn out if things go wrong in that person's life and you allow that to impact yours.

2. Do you have a pull to other people and a natural desire to help them?

Needless to say, the healing senses within will make you want to be more altruistic. If this has been a regular part of your life and you enjoy listening to people rant, you just might be an empath. There really isn't any downside to this as it's a win-win because helping people makes you feel good, but you should definitely be aware of people who try to take advantage of your philanthropic nature.

3. Are you suffering from sensing other people's emotions instead of your own?

Take a moment to sit and define whether or not the feelings you are experiencing are your own. The best way to do this is to remember or think about any time that you may feel sad or ecstatic for seemingly no reason at all. If this is a frequent occurrence and you have found yourself asking why you feel this way, you may be going through empathy.

When you are in such a moment, take a deep breath and ask yourself if that emotion came out of nowhere. Slow down and focus on yourself for a while, blocking those feelings out and bringing yourself back to earth in order to regain clarity. You need to be able to separate yourself from others or you may have a hard time.

4. Can you accurately read the mood of a room/area?

You'll definitely know if you're capable of doing this. An empath can simply walk into a room and immediately sense the energy of it. If you're one of those people who have a knack for aptly picking up the vibe of others around you, you sound like an empath to me.

If you want to give this a test, give yourself a moment to take in your surroundings next time there are other people around. If you feel like you know how someone is feeling, don't be afraid to casually ask them how they're doing. Should your inclination be correct based on their answer, that's a sign that you're empathic by nature.

Upon discovering this, you might be more attuned than ever to their vibe. If it's a negative one, you should probably keep the interaction short and sweet. You don't want to open yourself up to unwanted energy. As an emotional sponge of sorts, you should practice self-care the second you start to feel out of it.

5. Do you find public places overwhelming?

This relates to the previous question. Social gatherings, loud events, and crowded places can be over-stimulating. You'll find that it's a problem for you because you're focused on the outside influences rather than yourself. If that's the case, it's yet another clue.

6. Does spending time around people drain you?

Now, this one is a bit complicated. Alone, it could be a sign that you're simply an introvert. In conjunction with everything else, however, you could take it as a sign. See, many empaths are introverted because they recharge when they're on their own. Being introverted alone doesn't make you an empath though.

If you are someone who feels down after spending time with other people or even *while* you are with them, you might be an empath. The reason this happens is because you're surrounded by all those emotions. You never know what another person is going through until you feel it yourself, an unfortunate side-effect of being an empath.

7. *Are you able to manage being around negative and/or toxic people?*

Look, the world is full of unhealthy humans who *can* and *will* bring you down if they're given half the chance. Empaths are caring by nature and so, they avoid these people as much as they possibly can. These relationships are unhealthy because they can impact your wellbeing.

Regardless of what the situation might be, it's best that you get out of it. It could be a relationship like that of one with a coworker, but sometimes we need to sacrifice our jobs for our mental health. Your health is the most important thing, always.

8. Are you extremely creative?

Most empaths go into artistic fields of work or they partake in them and the beauty of nature whenever they have free time. As a result, you may be one of the people who avoids the corporate culture, not because you don't find it interesting but because the cut-throat job just isn't for you. You may be perfectly capable of doing it, but it might cause you distress in the interim.

Another thing that would bother you about the corporate world is the lack of quiet. Things are always noisy and sometimes manipulative in that world. If this doesn't appeal to you, you may be an empath, and it's important for you to create a space for your creativity so that you can pursue your passions and make the most out of enjoying your life.

9. How often do you feel scattered?

If you haven't learned to hone the gift of being an empath, you may find that your thoughts are hazy and unclear. This comes from a state of being overwhelmed because you are engulfed by the emotions and feelings of others, making you disconnect from yourself. Zoning out is a symptom of this mentality.

Setting up proper boundaries is a good way to help you move past this feeling. You'll think clearer if you reconnect with your own thoughts and feelings. Once again, meditation is a good form of self-care that can help you accomplish this one when you need it most.

10. Are you an overly and/or extremely emotional person?

Usually, but not always, empaths are easy criers. There are many mental illnesses such as anxiety and depression that can make you feel supremely sensitive, but if it's a regular occurrence and no amount of treatment seems to solve it, you may be an empath. This is one of the reasons so many empaths tend to avoid things like media; their hearts are so big that they'll find themselves crying at any sort of injustice, fiction or otherwise.

Empaths feel the pain quite literally, whereas most people simply grow upset or uncomfortable with such media depictions. Afterward, if you need to, take the time to detach from the things that made you feel this way. Make an active attempt not to let this sort of thing get to you.

Protection Phase

Let's be real for a moment. The world in its current climate of expression is a terrible place for an empath. There are several things that can negatively impact an empath today, and we're obviously going to feel large amounts of sympathy as a result. With the world in this state, it makes applying reason to external situations important so that we can make good decisions.

There are many healthcare professionals that become hard because of empathizing too much. This can make their patients feel like they are uncaring. This is usually due to over protecting themselves against empathy overloads.

The best way to avoid reaching this point is by grounding yourself and putting your own feelings and emotions above the pain of others—though I know that is easier said than done.

Setting Boundaries and Emotional Controls

It's easy to lose track of yourself if you become what is known as an empathic chameleon. What this means is that you are the type of empath who adjusts the way they behave when around certain people in order to make those people feel more at ease around you. It's imperative not to let yourself become disassociated in this process.

There are several practices you can perform in order to protect yourself as an empath. These are great for lessening the problems of being an empath. You'll be able to use these to take advantage of your gift.

The essential practices are:

- Develop a shield-self: This sounds a little weird and you may want to look into finding someone who can teach you how to do this, but this means using your aura and outer energy to shield yourself. You literally visualize a shield of energy around yourself, one that is complete and impenetrable. You might like to choose a specific color that works for you and picture the shield this way. This shield is meant to be alive, flowing and moving with life so that it is flexible. When it is flexible, you can use it to serve you rather than block *everything* out. If you do this exercise on a regular basis, you will master it.

- Try not to lose yourself: When you are alone, try to bring yourself back to yourself by focusing on all your own feelings and thoughts. This is an act of centering yourself in order not to lose yourself to the sensations that surround you. After some time, you should be able to do this around other people. This should eventually work almost like a switch where you can acutely feel the difference between yourself and your environment. It helps to concentrate on the differences between the two so that you can always remind yourself what it feels like to simply be you with yourself.

- Take responsibility for you and only you: It is not your job to fix everyone around you. I know that it is something you can grow used to, but it's important not to break the boundaries between sanity and insanity. You might know exactly where your line is as an empath. Try not to go any further than that line. If you don't already know where it is, it may be best for you to try and figure that out. This will help you maintain better, more stable relationships in the long-run. It also means that you will avoid toxic relationships and friendships.

- Don't try to fix everything: Empaths can come across as saintly to other people. I know how hard it is to be known as the "nice guy" in the room because you're so caring and kind all the time. There will be people who feed off of that energy, but it is vital that you remain true to yourself. The reason is because lying for the sake of protecting someone's feelings stops others from growing up. Sometimes we have to be the bad guy and tell these people how we really feel in order to break them out of their padded reality. They may hate you at first or grow to believe that you are not the nice person they thought you were, but they will thank you for it in the long-run. You need to look honestly at the mirror in order to improve yourself and so do other people. Don't be afraid of showing someone their true reflection.

- Practice healthy living: I know I'm probably beginning to sound like a broken record, but I cannot stress the importance of taking care of yourself. You need to do this in more than an emotional/mental space. Physical self-care is something too often overlooked by most people. There are several things that you should do regularly and most of them are obvious. Still, I'm going to share them anyway.

- Sleep and sleep *often*: I know that the outside influences can keep you up at night, but if you are sleep-deprived, you are going to awaken a load of side effects including insomnia and a weakened immune system. Empaths are already prone to light sleeping. It's best not to make things worse, so try to get at least six hours of sleep and create a sleeping habit.
- Eat healthily and get some exercise: I'm not telling you to join a gym, although that couldn't hurt, but at least take a short walk every day and make sure you aren't living off of junk food. It will aid in a more positive outlook on your life if you feed your body with healthy fuel like the essential vitamins and minerals that you need.

- Clean: No one likes cleaning, right? Well, the cleaner your environment, the clearer your mind will feel. This doesn't go just for the exterior either. Good ways of clearing your mind are spending time in solitude, showering, or taking leisurely baths whenever you are able.

Social Protection from Narcissistic Abuse and Energy Vampires

When I first heard the term, I found myself wondering what energy vampires were. As it is, they're exactly what they sound like. Rather than sucking the life force out of you via blood, they do so via energy. Although empaths are kind-hearted and generally quite tolerant, they do not enjoy being around people who do not think of others. Since this is what an empath does by nature, it's important for them to stay away from arrogant, egotistical, and narcissistic people. These are the type of people who can bring an empath down to the point where even sleep will not cure the tiredness they feel.

Empaths are naturally likable, and they have a bit of a people-pleasing mentality that comes from being as sensitive as they are, so whilst it's cool to make people feel good because it makes you feel good too, sometimes empaths are going to come across someone who simply chooses to be miserable. You know what they say; misery loves its company and who better to share in misery than an empath who has little choice in the matter? No matter how hard you try to change it, there are people who enjoy being negative and if you allow them to, these people will drag you down. This person can bring out the worst in you—they might make you gossip, fight, or complain all the time even if these things are not inherent to your usual behavior.

It is up to you to stop yourself from slipping into this downward spiral.

The compassion and love of an empath are definitely ones that can heal, but this does nothing to change a narcissist. You cannot change the negative behaviors of this person. To try is to waste your time and your energy. They do not appreciate you or anyone else for that matter, nor do they appreciate all that others do for them. If you have ever been in a relationship with one of these people, you know exactly what I am talking about. If you haven't, I implore you to avoid trying to show them how deeply you love them. Though yours is conditional, theirs is nothing but greed for the unique love you are offering to them. They know this is not the ordinary, and they will use it for as long as you allow them to.

You see, narcissists are entitled. They believe that you owe them your devotion. Unfortunately, they consider this disposable and will gladly toss it and you away once they are done siphoning all the compassion they can from you.

It's important to come to terms with the fact that being an empath does not mean you should always forgive someone for their actions. You are not a doormat. The love you have to give should be appreciated by someone who understands exactly how valuable it is. Empaths can be destroyed by narcissists due to mistaking a narcissist for someone who can actually be healed. Incidentally, narcissists are the type of people who immediately enter into new relationships after theirs end. This is usually because that other person has been there in the background the entire time.

If you have ever been in a relationship with this type of person or feel like you currently are, trust me when I say that you are not alone. As sad as it is, this kind of relationship is the type that makes you set boundaries in place, and that is a good thing. However; if you are unused to implementing boundaries, it can be a difficult process to begin.

Are They Narcissists?

It's a rather unfortunate circumstance that negativity is always stronger than positivity. Optimists try to be positive, but it is harder to be confident in that feeling when pessimism can so easily resemble realism. This is why you should work on improving your self-confidence. If you are truly focused on your beliefs, to the point that no one can sway you from your opinion, you will be undefeatable.

One of the best ways to respond to negativity is with understanding and support. It's easy to dismiss someone's negativity because you don't want it to overwhelm you, but that person is feeling upset in one way or another. You don't need to validate these feelings in order to offer your compassion. At that moment, that is their truth.

Narcissists believe that they are perfection

embodied, but in all honesty, no one is perfect. That's what makes us human. I know I've been telling you that it's important to practice self-care, but that doesn't mean that you shouldn't take risks. You can still live your life and enjoy it while taking care of yourself. Our life only lasts so long, and while you are here, you have the opportunity to change things. You may have found yourself with a narcissist and that can be enough to put anyone off wanting to get to know other people, but at least you experienced what it was like to love someone.

Don't let this turn you away from experiences altogether. Learn from it. Don't lose yourself to protecting yourself from people with flaws. People will always have flaws. In the end, resisting everyone and everything won't help you on your journey to finding happiness.

These are some of the character traits that narcissists show, and if you see any of these, it is better that you avoid those people altogether:

- They are authoritative: Narcissists have the tendency to be bossy. This is because they feel like they are good at everything.

- They can be quite manipulative when they want to be: They generally want you to do what they want, as their bossiness would suggest, and so they will try to trick you into doing it. They have a sick love of exploiting people because their own interests come above those of others.

- They have a need for admiration, devotion, and/or adoration: A narcissist craves the sense of admiration and devotion they can only get from others. They feed their own ego by constantly talking about their own personal achievements to the point where they make others think less of themselves.

- They are entitled: This kind of goes without saying once you take a look at the other points I've listed. They believe that, somehow, others owe them due to their heightened sense of self-righteousness and arrogance.

- They lack empathy: This one goes without saying, but I'm going to say it anyway because I want this to be very clear. Narcissists are empty, bankrupt souls. They do not show a hint of emotion or feeling to anyone or anything. This would make them vulnerable, and that isn't something they're prepared to be. They consider it weakness, and it would put them beneath you or bring them down to your level. This is why they must be avoided at all costs. Empaths don't need that kind of energy coming anywhere near them.

Part Three:

Unleash Your Full Potential

Use Your Gift to Thrive in Life

By this point in the book, we have determined that being an empath is indeed a wonderful gift to have. However, it can be mentally and emotionally draining if one doesn't take proper care of oneself. There are certain ways to do this.

It might not always seem like it is possible, but it is important to have coping methods that help keep you physically *and* mentally healthy through the daily struggles you have to face. That's the part that most people forget about: the mental side of things. Your mind is as important as your body—in fact, sometimes it's more important. One of the many daily struggles empaths have to deal with is the constant flow of energy and emotions from the people all around them.

In this part of the book, we will journey on a path of self-improvement. Why is self-improvement relevant, you ask? In this case, it will help you develop a positive mindset. This, in turn, will allow you to regain self-confidence by focusing on the positive aspects of your gift. You can use it to thrive, rather than allow it to bring you down.

Understanding and Controlling Your Emotions

Emotions are one of the driving forces in everyone's life. We all have them and they have seen us through many things, no matter who we are or how old we are. They were there when we went through devastating and painful heartbreaks, when we faced and survived some of our biggest fears, and when we needed the warning to move away from toxic situations. Of course, they aren't only there during the bad times. They've given us the ability to feel the joys of true friendship, compassion for one another, and one of the strongest emotions of them all, to love as deeply as we can.

It's easy to let emotions lead the way, especially when one considers how strong and powerful they can be, but these feelings should always be met with reason and logic. That seems a tough one to think about, doesn't it? Emotional control is something not often heard of.

That being said, emotional control is a term I've heard a lot throughout my life. My mother, in particular, was the one who taught me about EQ. As an empath, it was something I often lost sight of by becoming too emotionally invested and/or involved. As a result, I often let my emotions rule me when I should have been ruling them. So, what exactly is EQ?

We all know what IQ is, right? Well, EQ is basically the emotional equivalent, being our emotional intelligence. Identifying and strengthening our EQ helps to enable us to control our emotions. It's the ability to recognize not only our own emotions, but the emotions of others. We know empaths are especially good at feeling the emotions of others, but they aren't always good at telling the difference between these feelings and appropriately naming them, along with separating their own emotions from the emotions of others. That's why it's important to develop and understand EQ because you can use these feelings and emotions as a guide to manage and/or adjust emotions. Once you've learned to manage them, you'll be better equipped to adapt to environments, achieve your goals, and behave/think more appropriately in any given situation.

Having a good level of control over your emotions doesn't mean that you can't fall head over heels in love or that you can't have a bit of a mental breakdown every now and then. We are all human, after all. These are totally normal experiences to go through. That being said, there are certain emotions such as jealousy and anger that cause us to lose a fair bit of logic and reasonable thinking. This is where learning how to handle those negative emotions comes into play. If we don't handle them correctly, they could spiral out of control and pull us further down into a pit of negativity.

So, how do we become emotionally stronger and avoid disaster? I'm going to go through a few techniques on how to do exactly that below. These methods will also help make you more mentally stronger than ever before.

Use Your Body Language

Body language is the expressive nonverbal form of communication through body movements, facial expressions, and gestures. In general, our body language is a sequence of subconscious actions that portray our internal reaction to different situations. As with actual language, the way we move can show others how we feel and what we are thinking, just as we can learn what others are feeling and thinking based on the way they move.

How you communicate through movement and gestures is important. It can sometimes give away your true thoughts and emotions more honestly than a verbal reaction can because we often don't even mean to react in certain ways. The movement of the body is natural. The gestures we make don't need to be thought about. The way we raise our eyebrows is not something we consider doing beforehand.

Understanding body language is what makes it easier for us to pick up on how others react and feel toward us. Have you ever experienced someone constantly looking away or being easily distracted during a conversation? They just don't seem very interested in what you have to say, do they? Are there other times you can keep eye contact so long during an engaging conversation that you forget to blink? There is no "correct" way to use body language but by being more fluid and relaxed with yourself and your body's movements, you can portray more positive reactions and can even make yourself more approachable. Take posture as another example; if you're uncomfortable in a social situation, you're more likely to tense up. To appear more comfortable, you can keep your head up straight while relaxing your shoulders. These simple gestures can give off the appearance that you are more at ease, even if you are experiencing stress at that point in time.

Being aware of your own movements and gestures is a good way to try keep your emotions hidden and under control. Of course, it's not good to keep things bottled up, but as an empath, you don't want your heavy burden of feelings and emotions to flow out in certain situations. Stay strong and keep your head up. You know as well as I do that these negative emotions are fleeting. If you don't let them get to you and don't let others know that they're getting to you, you'll find that they are easier to release at the end of the day.

Use Positive Thinking

With so much negative energy in the world, it is often difficult to practice positive thinking.

Positive thinking starts with self-talk. Self-talk is easy enough to identify. It's the voice in all of our minds and the constant chain of thoughts that the voice repeats on a daily basis. Unfortunately, these thoughts are vulnerable to negativity and can lead you down the path of pessimism if you spend too long stuck inside your own head. This path is full of self-doubt and stress which, evidently, a sensitive empath—or anyone for that matter—does not need in their life. Therefore, we need to turn that voice into a positive one instead. Training yourself to have positive thoughts is better for your overall health; it can reduce stress levels and help you cope better in difficult situations. However; this mental training takes time because it always takes time to break any old habit.

Try appreciating and searching for humor during the day to lighten your mood. Be gentle and rational with yourself during the day by evaluating what you are really thinking and consider if it is positive or negative. Stop and take a deep breath whenever you catch those thoughts. Consider whether or not they are necessary or valid. If they aren't, turn them onto a new path. You may want to consider meditation as meditation is a fantastic way to train the mind to let go of thoughts, treating them like clouds that drift across the sky. You take note of these, but then you let them pass on by because you have no other choice. Surround yourself with positive and supportive people. It is much easier to forget and let go of the bad thoughts when in company of good friends who make you laugh more than anything else.

Remember that anything can have a positive twist to it if you try hard enough. After all, this can only benefit your emotional health. Positivity is not ignoring life's problems; it is taking these issues and turning them around to make the best of a bad situation.

You might drop the birthday cake at a big party, but simply because the beautiful icing was destroyed doesn't mean that it is inedible. It could be a story you look back at with a smile. It all depends on the way you react to the situation.

Use Positive Speaking

Words are one of the most powerful forces in the world, and they are conducted by one of the smallest organs of the human body. We don't always realize it, but what we speak out into the world does have an influence. Subconsciously, we follow what we hear. Think about what you're projecting out into the world; does it have a positive or negative impact on your life?

When you speak negatively, it only breeds more negative energy and can create fear and hopelessness. Sometimes it can worsen anxiety and other mental states such as depression and panic. Remember, your mental health is vastly important and relates directly to your emotional health.

People perceive you not only by the way you speak, but also how you speak of yourself and others. We've all been in situations where we've either been gossiped about or criticized too harshly. These situations can easily be ignored, but most of the time, they do hurt us.

Whilst these terrible words and judgments can impact us enormously, positive speaking has just as much power. Through it, we can show love, our consideration for one another, and create reassurance where it is most needed.

Words are also a way to express your emotional overload, and simply talking about how you feel can be one of the biggest stress relievers. That being said, you need to be aware that it is unhealthy to complain all the time. As with positive thinking, you have the choice of how to look at your life. If you are constantly complaining, people will see you as a person who constantly complains. However, if you try to say something good every time you speak to someone, they'll remember that about you and so will you.

Evaluate your speech in the future and remember that positive speaking can definitely influence your emotions. Change your tone of voice if necessary. Let others know how you feel and use your words to embody who you are. If you want to be a positive person, it's up to you to make that happen. And if you want to release the negativity holding you back, you can do so with practice.

Create Your Own Personal Space

Is there a certain space you love, a place you can go where you can ponder over all your thoughts and feelings and feel safe and secure? It may be curled up in bed, or a spot in your favorite coffee shop, or a quiet corner of your local library. There are many possibilities. When we mention or talk about our own personal space, that's the type of image that comes to mind. That place of comfort and relaxation that belongs to you and only you, the one you might have thought of first, is your space. However, in this case, such a space is much more complex than a mere adored location.

Your own personal space is one that you set the boundaries for. You get to decide what goes and what doesn't. We set boundaries in place to protect ourselves both physically and emotionally. It's our own comfort zone where we can keep things at a distance, whether it's during a physical or emotional interaction. Within this space, the act of overstepping a boundary can be anything that makes you uncomfortable in any way, be it someone being too loud around you when you don't like loud noise, someone sitting too close to you, or even a partner or friend wanting you to reveal something personal that you aren't willing to share. It's important to set these boundaries and stick to them. Any issues regarding them should be treated with care and seriousness, rather than being shrugged off.

When your personal space is compromised you

might feel drained, agitated, or upset with yourself for being angry and/or hurt. You might not even know the reason why you're reacting this way, especially if you haven't identified what your boundaries are. Your self-esteem might come crashing down due to this simple fact, which can hurt your confidence. Overstepping boundaries is a form of violation. Some cases may be more intense than others, but they remain the same no matter how big or small your boundaries. It is important to define them for yourself.

We all have different needs and ideas of personal space. It is important to remember that it is okay to want your own. It is indeed personal, and it's perfectly all right to want that. Never feel bad for maybe needing more space than others. The important thing is that you acknowledge that you need it. We all do at times. Be clear, firm, and polite when explaining what your personal space is to people. Hopefully they will respect you enough to accept them. In any circumstance where this does not happen, it is probably better to move on from the person and the situation. Your beautiful self does not deserve to be disrespected in that way.

That respect starts first with yourself. Respect yourself enough not to give in to pressure. It takes a lot of self-respect not to allow others to disrespect us.

Work on Time Management

Time management is crucial in our fast-paced lives. If we don't work on properly managing our time, we affect our emotions in adverse ways. An example of that includes that we stress and overwork ourselves, which can cause a storm of negativity. We're trying our best to avoid that negativity.

Now, some of us work best under pressure—which, to be honest, is not the best option—while others are more likely to start with their workload long in advance. Whichever way you choose to work, we are all prone to burn out. If we don't properly take care of ourselves, our time, and the amount of work we burden ourselves with, we can suffer from this. Believe me, burnout isn't fun. If you've never experienced it, be thankful and do your best never to reach that point. If you have, you'll know that you never want to experience it ever again.

Time management really is essential if you think about it. Our lives can't properly function without it. We would be late to appointments, overdue on work, and behind on bills to say the very least. So how are we supposed to manage it correctly?

Keep your thoughts clear and focus on the job at hand. Don't procrastinate. Where possible, avoid stress. That all sounds easy enough, doesn't it?

Now, of course if we could all avoid stress, we would. Stress usually causes our bodies and our minds to grow tired quickly, making everything seem a little heavier than usual. If our body is a wreck, our mind will feel the same way, and so too will our emotions. Above all else, it's best to take breaks. We all need a break sometimes. This doesn't mean that you should work yourself to a breaking point and then take time off. No, you need short breaks in between too. These can be a simple, regular break while working to help with those short spans of concentration. Make a cup of tea, close your eyes for five minutes, and maybe practice some breathing exercises.

In the end, it really is about finding what works best for you. Good time management is an ongoing and constant practice. Try to prioritize in advance to save yourself all the emotional drainage and stress. You can even work on these during those short breaks. If you work them into your everyday schedule, you might feel the stress you experience at the idea of a break start to slip away. It's all about working work *and* luxury into your schedule. Our bodies desperately require relaxation. Dedicating time to our mental and physical help can prevent burn out.

Confidence Is Key

Confidence is the belief in ourselves and what we are able to achieve. It gives us the ability to succeed in life and grab opportunities with both hands and without fear. Most importantly, it allows us to be accepting of ourselves and who we are. Other people can sense this just as empaths can sense it. Those who are more confident are often more approachable too.

There is a bit of a hefty line between too much and too little confidence. Overconfidence can make a person boastful, egotistical, and get them into difficult situations when they overestimate their abilities or think they are irreplaceable. The difference is basically arrogance verses self-confidence. On the other hand, having low confidence can hold you back a bit in life. You may not be willing to take that promotion you deserve or pursue a love interest even when the opportunities are laid out right in front of you. Low self-confidence can make you think that you aren't worthy of these things.

Having the right amount of confidence will help you tackle difficult challenges, build credibility, and create better relationships. We will go through how you can get your confidence back. In doing so, we'll look at ways to avoid emotional overloads and recognize the warning signs of such overloads.

Regaining Our Self-Confidence

Certain behaviors and beliefs are linked to how someone sees and values themselves. One such example is self-confidence. The more love, self-respect, and trust you build in yourself, the better for your overall self-esteem. It can easily be damaged through personal issues and unhealthy behaviors. If you work on these behaviors, you can prevent your self-esteem from taking a hit. Some of them are as simple as building healthy eating habits.

Empaths are more likely to suffer from low self-confidence than your average person as they tend to feel as if they're always the odd one out. Their highly sensitive natures make them vulnerable, and they are easily affected by emotions. Taking things to heart is not necessarily a bad thing; after all, that's exactly what makes an empath who they are. The emotional storms they often deal with are difficult at most times and can leave them feeling confused, angry, depressed, and can sometimes lead to anxiety and nervous disorders. These are all elements that contribute to your self-esteem.

Does this mean that if you're an empath, you'll suffer from a lack of confidence? No, of course it doesn't. It simply means empaths are more prone to feeling that way than the rest of us. What does help is when you recognize that you are an empath (and not secretly crazy or deranged). Knowing what you are and what it means to be that would definitely help with self-esteem. You can immediately eliminate some self-doubt and begin to appreciate yourself and your very special gift.

A good way to improve your self-confidence is to recognize what healthy elements there are to focus on. Being an empath isn't all bad. Have a clear view of your beliefs and morals. You need to be firm in what you believe in as this creates a sense of security. Whether you are religious or not, we all need something to believe in. If it's in yourself, you get the bonus of having ultimate security and confidence.

Do not fixate on past mistakes and constantly dwell on what you could have done differently; stay focused on the present and deal with what's happening at the current moment. Learning from your mistakes is still a valuable lesson, but you don't need to obsess over something to learn from it. Consider creating a list of positive affirmations to repeat to yourself whenever you feel like you're getting caught up in negative thoughts.

Try to have faith in yourself and don't compare yourself to others in any situation. You are beautifully, uniquely, and wonderfully made. With some time and effort and your new awareness of yourself, you are definitely on the path to regaining your self-confidence.

Overcoming Emotional Overloads and Negative Mindsets

For some of us, taking on our own emotional loads and those of others tends to be a terrible habit. However, as an empath, how is it possible to feel so deeply and avoid being exhausted and overwhelmed? It is not an easy task, I can guarantee you, but it is possible.

Anxiety can be one of the main causes of emotional overload for an empath. Having anxiety means you stress about everyone and everything, and by everything, I do mean everything. These excessive anxious thoughts can cause a great amount of negativity and lead to an emotional overload. During these moments, consider simple meditation skills to clear your mind for a few minutes and give yourself a chance to breathe. In extreme cases, medical help may be necessary to control your anxiety. Don't let it stand in your way of living your life to the fullest.

Don't run away from your pain or stress. We tend to want to ignore what we're dealing with and convince ourselves that we're okay when clearly, we are not okay. All you're doing by avoiding issues is building up more emotional stress. You cannot escape it, so be kind to yourself and let it all out. Sit down, let the emotions flow, and accept how you're feeling. Once you've done this, you can then try and deal with the situation at hand and move on. Ignoring it will not fix anything. Instead, accepting the way you're feeling and the position you're in can lead you to the next step. Once you know where you are at mentally and emotionally, you can ask yourself how to get out of that situation and/or how to deal with it. Follow the logic and reason we spoke about earlier.

As much as we want the world to be a better place, you cannot fix everyone. When someone that an empath cares about is going through a rough time, the empath will obviously feel the burden of the struggles themselves. Remember that there is only so much you can do to help someone. Don't beat yourself up about not being able to do anything about the situation. Sometimes the only thing you can do is to be there for someone. Don't cause yourself all the unnecessary stress and pain of taking the situation onto yourself. If you really can help, then do so by all means. However; if you can't, the best thing you can do for both of you is to be a supportive structure for them and leave it at that.

Question your thoughts and reasons for your stress. Are you stressing about something that is happening or are you stressing about something that might happen? If it's something that might happen, take a step backward and let those worries go because stressing about the "what if" is only going to lead into a downward spiral. Are you anxious about yourself or someone else's feelings? If it's someone else, you need to take a deep breath and think about what you can do for them because there is no way you'll be any help to anyone else if you're freaking out as much as they are. Are your thoughts negative or positive? If they're negative, I can guarantee you they're just upsetting and stressing you out even more, so you need to release those negative thoughts and change their direction to a more positive path.

Don't make mountains out of molehills, and remember when you stress about something before it happens, you're only causing yourself more emotional strain.

Stress Triggers and Coping Mechanisms

Stress is unfortunately just one of those things that is a part of our lives. There is no changing that, at least not at this point in time. If you are able to live an entirely stress-free life, I commend you. More often than not, however, we all have stressful lives, and we need to learn how to properly cope with them rather than attempt to eradicate stress altogether, since that may prove impossible. We put so much pressure on ourselves to be successful and perform well that we don't even notice the strain we're putting on ourselves until it is too late.

The funny thing is that stress can be both positive and negative. We can stress about wedding plans, fun events, or finding that perfect gift for a loved one, which are all considered positive things. However, stress can also protect us from dangerous situations like that stranger at the bar that stands a little too close for comfort. It's like our internal warning sign and listening to that warning sign can be a survival instinct.

We have a few different types of stress hormones that our bodies produce. What they do is build up a type of memory to keep us away from upsetting and dangerous situations. These hormones can be helpful in small doses, but when released in abundance one can suffer from depression, weakened memory, and low attention span. It is for this reason that we need to try our best to avoid stress becoming too much.

We all have different triggers of stress, and we have to identify them in order to recover and heal ourselves.

Reorganize your life and declutter. By reorganizing, you may gain a clearer image of what's causing you so much stress, and you can make a plan to remove it from your life. Decluttering physical space can give you better space and a clean environment to thrive in.

There's a reason why feng shui is so popular. Consider reading up on it and using it to improve your space. You may find all your worries fading away and being replaced with positivity.

Prioritizing can also help you decide what the most important elements of your life are. By focusing on these elements, you eliminate other trivial matters that can be triggering your stress levels. In other words, you may be worried about the speck of dust on the television when you bring guests home, whereas they probably don't even notice it at all. In such an instance, you are causing yourself unnecessary stress. When you are stressed and overwhelmed, think of your priorities and remember you are busy working on the most important factors of your life.

There are some daily activities to consider that can help you get rid of all the negative energy and stress. Writing or journaling is a good way to get your thoughts out on paper, successfully removing them from your mind and allowing them not to clog up your thoughts. Running, jogging, singing, and dancing are all very expressive, and exercise is known to release stress due to activating serotonin and dopamine levels. These are two hormones that make us happy.

You have to get in touch with what your body and mind need. Stress is a method that your body uses to scream at you to pay attention to it, and it is all too often ignored. It is your job to take care of and nurture yourself.

The Positive Aspects of the Gift of Empathy

We all have natural gifts and talents. Some individuals are artistic, some are sporty or adventurous, and some are empaths. No gift should ever be hidden; following your passions is a way of finding purpose in life, which is something we all need to thrive. Consider some abilities that your gift has given you that you maybe weren't even aware of.

Empathetic Listening

Empathetic listening is truly understanding and being able to perceive what someone is saying to you. There is absolutely no judgment involved, but only raw compassion and understanding. Empathetic listening is not always easy as it means putting all your own personal needs and opinions aside to focus on who really needs your support. It's not necessarily about giving advice but about lending an ear to someone in need. Empaths are able to do this far easier than others, and, in fact, many empaths become psychologists and counselors because of it.

How comforting is the thought of having a space to release your emotions in a safe environment? This is exactly what someone with the gift of empathetic listening provides. It requires a certain level of thoughtfulness between the two individuals involved and can definitely create a bond. Through using their gift, empaths improve their ability to understand and console, which strengthens them in many aspects of their lives.

Attentiveness is given to what is being said, and this will make the individual feel important and cared for. It releases tension and can improve the mood, which is one of the things an empath lives for. The other person won't have to worry about being interrupted while releasing your emotions as an empathetic listener will constantly reassure them during the process. When someone's needs are put first and acknowledged, it increases their confidence and will forge a positive light on speaking up about how they feel in the future. It can never be a bad thing to be able to openly and honestly voice your thoughts.

Through empathetic listening, an empath can truly help someone in need. This is definitely a gift to be proud of. Use it often and you will never be without loved ones.

Empathetic Leading

Empathetic leading is sometimes viewed as a weak trait, but this is most definitely not the case. To be a good leader, sometimes it is required that you be able to put yourself in the other person's shoes for a moment. Empathetic leaders are also generally empathetic listeners as it is beneficial to them to be able to intently listen and understand the needs of those around them. Empaths that are in charge of others mostly don't have the "do as I say" attitude and are emotional thinkers which might seem like a poor skill to some, but in fact, is a unique kind of strength. If there is one thing that people being led by someone else want to feel, it is equality. Empathetic leaders make those around them feel like equals by considering them in every aspect of decision-making.

Empathetic leaders can use their gift to their advantage in more ways than one. They are able to suss out the bad apples and pick up on some things that may be sketchy. They might even use the knowledge of someone else's feelings and emotions in a way that is beneficial to them if they deem it necessary.

The gift of being an empathetic leader is that those under you are likely to truly respect you and your opinions. It creates loyalty and clear communication, which helps to improve overall work ethic. The ability to put yourself in someone else's shoes is a fantastic one.

Empathetic Relationships

No relationship is ever perfect. For one to succeed, it requires effort from each partner, many sacrifices, and a lot of forgiveness. Above all else, you need to be able to compromise. If your partner is an empath, you may be much luckier than you think. They can be very difficult people to understand and deal with at times, but they have the traits that make up some of the best life partners.

Empaths are unbelievably loyal to their loved ones. They only wish to see the best in their partners, and they will give their partners their whole heart and soul. You see, when empaths dedicate themselves to something, they go all in. This includes relationships. You will be the main focus point in their lives, and they will do anything to make sure you know that you are loved and cared for. They are the type of people that will move mountains even if all they get back in return is a smile. Once they have devoted themselves to you, they will love unconditionally. This love is one of the purest forms you will ever find.

Since an empath's emotions and feelings are so intense, they are able to love just as deeply. They feel very passionately and will never deliberately hurt you as it would cause them great upset. They can often use their gift to read the situation and get a gauge on how you are feeling. When angry, they are very careful when selecting their words as they will not say anything to worsen a situation because their gift allows them to understand the situation on a deeper level. Openness and honesty are high up on the list of what empaths find important, and when they trust you, they will not do anything to hide their thoughts and fears from you. They are able to bring out the best in you through their joy and happiness and the optimism is only beneficial in a partner's life.

When an empath feels the pain of their partner,

their natural healing instincts will come out, and they will do anything to subdue the pain and protect you. Some may not realize it, but with an empath by your side, you will possess the ability to make the world a better place. They are able to understand you on a different level due to their amazing ability to feel what you are feeling.

Change Your Mindset

I believe that success and happiness are all about our mindsets. It affects everything in our lives, even how we react and handle the world around us. To achieve your goals, you need your mindset to level up with your aspirations.

The Path to Self-Improvement

Your self-talk has a direct connection with whether or not you have a positive or negative mindset. Consider changing your negative self-talk into a full-on empowerment speech. Who better to encourage you than yourself? It'll have the biggest impact. One of the ways you can do this is by using the positive affirmations I mentioned earlier.

Your mindset is also a reflection of how you see yourself. If you constantly believe, for example, that you're a slob or a bad worker, you will eventually train your brain into believing and following these thoughts. Through reading, you might be surprised at how quickly you pick up on the author's way of thinking. Look into some literature that will lead you in the right direction and try to avoid dark and heavy reading until you're in a better headspace. Reading is an excellent activity for an empath to take up due to their ability to see how others feel and think. You may find that books help you feel more positive, depending on their genres and titles. Go for self-motivating and happy books and take note of how much your mindset changes by journaling.

Using your environment to exercise your way of thinking is maybe one of the best options for an empath. We tend to forget that there is a lot more out there than little old us when trapped in a certain mindset. You might think you're stuck in the worst situation possible until you see someone else in an even worse predicament than yourself. Nature can be your getaway and "mind cleanser" when you really need it. There is nothing like beautiful scenery to readjust your way of thinking and make you appreciate the beauty of this world and life. As a bonus, sunshine is fantastic for a natural mood-booster. Once your head is clear again, you can carry on with your self-improvement journey. Sometimes all we need is a bit of a break from our own minds in order to get back on track. There's no better break than a walk in nature. You could even take that book along.

Surround yourself with people that have your desired mindset and try to celebrate your daily small achievements in life; it will lead you to accomplishing many more.

You Are Good Enough

Trust me, everyone on the planet has had a moment where they felt like they weren't good enough. Worse than that, I believe all of us have let the words and thoughts of others dictate how we feel about ourselves. No one can make you feel that way if you do not let them. Ultimately, you are in charge of your feelings and thoughts. Do not let anyone take that away from you.

A perfect example of what can make us feel like we're not good enough is the opinions of others and that little voice in our own head.

Shut down your inner critic. He's not doing you any good. You can talk back. The moment that little voice starts nagging at you about something that makes you feel inferior, shut it down. By shifting your focus onto something else or just simply saying "no," you are training yourself to recognize your self-worth. Make a list of what boosts your confidence on those days that you just aren't able to get rid of that voice. Perhaps you should consider saving or writing down messages that someone said that put a smile on your face. If they're truly worth it, stick them up somewhere you'll see them often, like the bathroom mirror.

It is so easy to compare ourselves to others on a daily basis as we always want to be the best that we can possibly be. The hard truth is that there is always going to be someone better than you. There will always be someone smarter, faster, or more attractive. You need to make peace with it or it will eat you up inside. You don't need to be better than everyone else. You only need to be you. Trust me, being you is a pretty great thing. Being the best you is what is important, not being better than someone else.

Social media is one of the things that is a major cause of people not feeling good enough about themselves. Many of us have at least one social media account and it is incredibly difficult to avoid, particularly since they are designed to be addictive. We so easily compare ourselves to a picture-perfect life online while completely ignoring the fact that we all have our flaws and rough days. Just because someone is more likely to share their fun and exciting days online doesn't mean there aren't bad ones they don't show you. Let go of the unrealistic idea that everything is perfect for anyone who isn't you.

Do things that make you happy and make you feel good. Compliment that stranger on their shoes if you really want to. If you make them feel good, you're bound to make yourself feel even better. I don't know about you, but I love making other people smile. Just be kinder to yourself and know that being human is about being flawed. It's not something to put yourself down over.

Stop Procrastinating

Oh procrastination, how much more would we get done without you in our lives.

I'm going to tell you, my humble reader, a secret. If you want to make changes in your life, it's up to you to do it. You need to put aside all those reasons not to because in truth, there really isn't a reason at all. Stop procrastinating. Make the changes.

Aim for your desired direction of change and go for it. Choose the fruit salad over those biscuits that are seductively whispering sweet nothings in your ear. Cut off that toxic person that causes nothing but upset in your life. These are some of the most important first steps into realizing your full self-worth. You know yourself better than anyone, even if it doesn't always feel like it. If you want to do something or your mind is telling you to do something, there is probably a good reason for it.

Of course this is not as easy as it sounds; it requires hard work and dedication. To start off, pick one personal change that seems most important to you and aim for it. Remember that even baby steps are better than standing still. Write down your progress to keep yourself motivated and to be able to reflect on how far you've come. Be patient. As with all good things in life, it will take time to make these changes, so don't get discouraged when things don't happen immediately. Nobody else will be able to take the first steps for you, but once you begin, you'll realize how much you're really worth it.

And believe me, you *are* worth it.

Conclusion

Well, we've reached the end. By this point, you know what empaths are and what kinds of empaths there are. They're special individuals born with different variations in their nervous system that make them ultra-aware of the feelings and emotions of others. There are plenty of things to bear in mind with empaths, such as a higher degree of sensitivity, but you should now be aware of the fact that there is so much more to an empath.

My hope is that you have picked up some new skills from this book, like the ability to pick up on another person's body language and tone of voice. These are excellent in helping you understand others. An empath has likely always been able to pick up on another person's thoughts and emotions, whether they knew why or not, and I trust that the tips throughout this book will help empaths separate their own from others. As an act of self-preservation, it's important to be able to do that, though you can be there for another person. Their trauma is not yours. Always remember that.

Rather than absorb negativity and overwhelm

yourself with the emotions of others, be kind to yourself. Let go of these things. Take a deep breath and use the coping mechanisms I've given you to move on from them. If you let them burden you, they can go so far as to damage you physically. Practice self-care so as not to suffer from things like fatigue. If things ever get too much, it is okay to take a step back for yourself. As an empath, it can be incredibly difficult to take time for yourself, but you are under no obligation to fix everyone else.

This is a special gift. It is not something that can be developed or taught. You either are an empath or you aren't. It's something that you are born with, and no one can take that away from you. Embrace it. Learn to use these abilities and thrive in your life rather than let them drag you down. It's not every day someone can say they are an empath. Understand how truly unique that gift is.

Of course, it's better to learn the mechanisms to adapt early on in your life, but it's never too late to learn. I congratulate you on taking this journey of self-discovery, self-acceptance, and self-improvement. I hope that you will never stop taking steps forward because there is no such thing as over-improvement. With the proper education about your gift, you'll be less likely to resort to destruction and will be able to find healthier ways to cope.

Look, being an empath can feel like a curse and it's tough to remember all the good things about it. Hopefully this book has put your perspective on the gift in a good light because it truly is a gift. The next time you curse your heightened senses, creativity, and emotions, remember all the benefits you discovered in this book. It's an incredible thing to feel things so deeply and everyone loves creativity, even those who can't create things. Don't let anyone, including yourself, make you feel like those things aren't amazing.

If you focus on all the positive aspects of being an empath, there's another thing you'll be creating: a life where you use your gift to thrive. Yes, it really can help you thrive. You can do so much with this gift rather than let it weigh you down. Go out there and make the world a better place, starting with yourself. It's what we're here for.

Keep moving forward. Keep putting yourself in the shoes of others. Keep being you.

If you have any ideas you think I'd be interested in, feel free to tell me about them.

If you learned something valuable, I'd love to know all about it.

If you enjoyed this book, please leave a positive review.

Until next time, humble readers and fellow empaths.

References

"10 Big Benefits of Being an Empath," 2018. *Conscious Life News*. Retrieved 17 May 2019, from https://consciouslifenews.com/10-big-benefits-being-empath/11100753/

"10 Things You Never Realized Were The Side Effects Of Being An Empath," 2017. *SimpleCapacity*. Retrieved 17 May 2019, from https://simplecapacity.com/2017/12/10-things-you-never-realized-were-the-side-effects-of-being-an-empath/

"12 Signs You're an Empath & What to Do If You Are!" 2016. *Ask-Angels.com*. Retrieved 17 May 2019, from https://www.ask-angels.com/spiritual-guidance/traits-of-an-empath/

"30 traits of an Empath (How to know if you're an Empath)," 2013. *The Mind Unleashed*. Retrieved 17 May 2019, from https://themindunleashed.com/2013/10/30-traits-of-empath.html

"Being An Empath Will Basically Kill You Unless You Use These Tips," 2018. *The Daily Meditation*. Retrieved 17 May 2019, from https://www.thedailymeditation.com/highly-empathetic-person

Pursey, K., & Pursey, K. (2016). "6 Types of Empaths: Which One Are You and How to Make the Most of Your Gift?" *Learning Mind*. Retrieved 17 May 2019, from https://www.learning-mind.com/types-of-empaths/

Orloff, Judith (2019)."Are You an Empath? Take this 20 Question Empath Test." *Judith Orloff MD*. Retrieved 17 May 2019, from https://drjudithorloff.com/quizzes/empath-self-assessment-test/

Saeed, Kim (2019). "Empaths: How to Shield Yourself Against Narcissists." *Kim Saeed: Narcissistic Abuse Recovery Program*. Retrieved 17 May 2019, from https://kimsaeed.com/2019/03/19/empaths-how-to-shield-yourself-against-narcissists/

Steber, C. (2018). "11 Questions To Ask Yourself To Figure Out If You're An Empath." *Bustle*. Retrieved 17 May 2019, from https://www.bustle.com/p/11-questions-to-ask-yourself-to-figure-out-if-youre-empath-12167891

"Types of Empaths: Which One Are You?" 2018. *Thrive Talk*. Retrieved 17 May 2019, from https://www.thrivetalk.com/types-of-empaths/

"What's the Difference Between Empathy, Sympathy, and Compassion?" 2017. *The Chopra Center*. Retrieved 17 May 2019, from https://chopra.com/articles/whats-the-difference-between-empathy-sympathy-and-compassion

You, T. "Types of Empaths: 7 Real Life Lessons," 2018. *Depression Alliance.* Retrieved 17 May 2019, from https://www.depressionalliance.org/types-of-empaths/

Young, Scott H. (2009). "Honest Self-Evaluation." *Honest Self-Evaluation | Scott H Young. Scott H Young*. Retrieved 17 May 2019, from https://www.scotthyoung.com/blog/2009/03/12/honest-self-evaluation/

CPSIA information can be obtained
at www.ICGtesting.com
Printed in the USA
BVHW031605010520
579052BV00003B/926

9 781075 037528